Dracula Was a
LAWYER

Hundreds of Fascinating Facts
from the World of Law

Erin Barrett and
Jack Mingo

Foreword by David Colbert

D1007631

First published in 2000 by
Conari Press
Distributed by Red Wheel/Weiser, LLC
York Beach, ME
With offices at:
368 Congress Street
Boston, MA 02210
www.redwheelweiser.com

Cover Illustration: Colin Johnson

Cover and Book Design: Claudia Smelser

Author Photo: Jen Fariello

Library of Congress Cataloging-in-Publication Data

Barrett, Erin.
  Dracula was a lawyer : hundreds of fascinating facts from the
  world of law / Erin Barrett, Jack Mingo; foreword by David
  Colbert
     p.   cm. — (Totally riveting utterly entertaining trivia)
  Includes bibliographical references.
     ISBN: 1-57324-718-9 (alk. paper)
  1. Medicine—Anecdotes. 2. Mingo, Jack. II. Title.
  III. Series
K183.B37 2002
340'.092'2—dc21   2001005853

Printed in the United States of America on recycled paper.

05 04 03   Data Repro   10 9 8 7 6 5 4

Dracula Was a
LAWYER

Dracula Was a LAWYER

foreword

by **David Colbert**

editor of the *Eyewitness to America* series
and author of *The Magical Worlds of Harry Potter*

I, David Colbert, (hereinafter "the Forewordist") do swear, attest, declare, and affirm to you (hereinafter "the Reader" or, if the publisher and bookseller are lucky, "the Customer") that "this is a good book"—subject to the following conditions:

1. The word *this* applies only to the manuscript pages seen by the Forewordist, not any prior or subsequent editions or amendments made with or without my knowledge. The Forewordist takes no responsibility for changes made prior to printing unless they display exceptional editorial taste and skill.

2. Regarding the word *is,* the Forewordist relies on the precedent set by President (and lawyer) William Jefferson Clinton, who responded to questioning under oath with the mind-

bending, "That depends on what your definition of 'is' is."

3. It is understood by the Reader and/or Customer that "good" is a subjective opinion; furthermore, this paragraph will stand as notice that the Forewordist's subjective opinion is offered only regarding the use of the book as reading material; it is not to suggest that the book may be used as a foodstuff, or as legal tender for payment of debts, or to prop open doors, or to patch holes in an airplane wing. Any such use is neither intended nor authorized nor endorsed and is undertaken by the Reader or Customer strictly at his her own risk. Especially the bit about airplane wings.

4. Anyway, is it really a book? Bookstores sell empty journals and call them "blank books." What the heck is a "blank book"? Erin Barrett and Jack Mingo have spent decades (well, at least years—or months, maybe) digging up strangely fascinating trivia that will entertain and amuse (subject to local laws and restrictions), yet this volume shares a name with a

product that contains *absolutely no words whatsoever.* How can a consumer be assured something sold as a book will have words or pictures in it? How can writers and artists protect their rights? As an author himself, the Forewordist is outraged at this injustice, and feels compelled to respond as millions of citizens before him have done: *There oughtta be a law!*

On second thought . . .

Preface

Ever since laws first came into existence, there have been lawyers to write, interpret, defend, and (when necessary) circumvent them.

And almost from the beginning, everyone seemed to love to hate lawyers. There's the dark side of the law: the high fees, the long and convoluted contracts, the ability to twist the law and the truth in order to win a judgment. An old Jewish parable states, "Two farmers each claimed to own a certain cow. While one pulled on its head and the other pulled on its tail, the cow was milked by a lawyer."

Or what about Vlad the Impaler, also known as Dracula? He so believed in the law that he was willing to act simultaneously as the arresting officer, the prosecutor, and the defense lawyer for people who offended him. He'd offer a summation of their crime, then a defense . . . before leaving it up to Vlad the judge to pass judgment and Vlad the executioner to follow up on it.

To be fair, though, many lawyers have been

good men and women working for unpopular underdogs. For example, Mohandas Gandhi, the lawyer from India who led a nation to freedom. Or John Adams, an ardent patriot, who defended British soldiers who had fired into a mob during the Boston Massacre because he believed the soldiers deserved a fair trial. Or Adams's son, John Quincy Adams, who defended slaves who had commandeered a slave ship in a desperate attempt to find their own freedom.

No matter what your take is on the legal profession, we end with the words of author Charles Lamb: "Lawyers, I suppose, were children once." It's in this vein that we present this book for lawyers and the people who love them.

Erin Barrett
Jack Mingo

one

The Golden Oldies

You would expect a law against lawyers accepting *bribes,* but in 240 B.C., Rome passed a law prohibiting lawyers from accepting *fees.*

The punishment for tree mutilation in ancient Germany was death.

Speaking of strange laws, Puritans in the 1600s made it illegal for anyone to celebrate Christmas. They believed that gifts, carols, and decorations were incompatible with the Christian life, which should be plain and grim. (Considering what the holiday has since become, maybe they had the right idea.)

European colonists in nineteenth-century Brazil passed a law exempting "white people" from execution, no matter what their crimes. Authorities found a simple solution while following the letter of the law: they dyed condemned Caucasians blue before executing them.

By law, under Peter the Great, all Russian men sporting long whiskers had to pay special taxes on them.

Hey, now it can cost an arm and a leg! Hammurabi's Code of Law, enacted in 1780 B.C. in Babylon, dictated that a doctor found guilty of malpractice was to have his hands chopped off.

"The aim of the law is not to punish sins."

—*Justice Oliver Wendell Holmes*

We all scream for ice cream

The ice cream sundae is the ingenious concoction of a midwestern druggist who was trying to skirt the law. Blue Laws of the 1890s dictated that ice cream sodas were not to be served on Sunday because of the belief that soda water was an intoxicant. One creative fellow poured the flavored syrups straight over ice cream without any soda at all. It worked! People fell in love with a new—and legal—treat. In honor of the law that spawned it, the dessert was dubbed "Sunday," and eventually "Sundae."

Early on in baseball, Blue Laws were strictly followed: Baseball wasn't even played on Sunday until 1933. When the leagues did decide to play on Sunday, it wasn't because the laws were no longer in place. Scheduling demands simply made it worth ignoring or, if necessary, fighting the morality laws of the individual states.

The first record of the term "Blue Laws" was found in a 1762 anonymous pamphlet by the lengthy name of "The Real Advantages Which Ministers and People May Enjoy, Especially in the Colonies, by Conforming to the Church of England."

Why were morality laws called Blue Laws? Anglican minister and early colonist Samuel Peters brought the Blue Laws in Connecticut to light in England in his wildly erroneous book *General History of Connecticut* (1782). In it, Peters claimed these laws were called "blue" as a derivation on the phrase "bloody laws." This, of course, was pure bunk (as were most of the laws he claimed existed). Actually, it's believed they were called Blue Laws because the paper they were printed on may have been blue.

What were some of the completely fictitious Blue Laws listed in Samuel Peters' book? How about, "That no woman should kiss her child on Sabbath or Fasting-day," or "That every male should have his hair cut round, according to a cap." Also, "Married persons must live together or be imprisoned," and most shocking: "No food or lodging shall be afforded to a Quaker, Adamite, or other Heretic."

How Dry I Am

If you wanted to drink legally during Prohibition, you got "sick." The 18th Amendment prohibited the use of alcohol for "beverage purposes," but medicinal purposes were well within the law. Doctors liberally prescribed medicines containing alcohol.

"They can never repeal it," bragged Senator Andrew Volstead, regarding Prohibition in 1920s America. It was, thankfully, gone thirteen years later.

The 18th Amendment is the only constitutional amendment in American history that's been repealed. The 21st, therefore, is unique as well, in that it's the only amendment in history that exists for the sole purpose of repealing another.

Leaving Japan was strictly forbidden in the seventeenth century. Immigration into the country was also, for the most part, prohibited. Breaking the immigration laws was punishable by death.

People are surprised to hear that the southern state of Georgia passed the very first antilynching law in the United States in the late 1880s. The sentence for anyone breaking the law, however, was a mere four years in jail.

According to the books of silly laws, Oklahoma lawmakers placed a ban on whale hunting in any of the state's waters.

The U.S. Army once depended on camels to carry supplies for long distances through American deserts. A law making it illegal to hunt camels in Arizona is still on the books.

An early Poor Law on the slates of Connecticut once stated outright, "Any poor children who live idly or are exposed to want or distress" should be hauled off to work as apprentices until twenty-one if male and until eighteen or marriage if female. Giving children "honest labor" was considered charitable (well, profitable, too) prior to the twentieth century.

In 1925, the state of Tennessee prosecuted teacher John Scopes for the "crime" of teaching the theory of evolution in school. The law was not repealed until 1967, forty-three years after the famous legal battle.

During World War II, it was illegal in Germany to name a horse "Adolf."

In 1401, the English Parliament decreed, with violation of the law to be punished by burning alive, that no citizen may have a copy of the Bible in English.

The Red Flag Act (1836–1896) of England prevented all self-propelled vehicles from driving through town unless a man carrying a red flag preceded the vehicle. A lantern was to be used after dark. This law did what lawmakers had hoped: It virtually stopped all automobile traffic (and industry advancements, for that matter) until after 1896, when the law was changed.

The Vatican in 1139 outlawed crossbows for humanitarian reasons. The only exception being when used against Muslims.

The Scots, recognizing the archery was crucial for civil defense, outlawed golf in 1457 because they were afraid people were playing golf instead of practicing for war. They did it again during WW II, needing the raw materials that were being used to manufacture golf balls.

In France it was once strictly against ordinance to mention Napoleon's favorite flower—the violet—in public.

In Chicago, home of many major pinball manufacturers, playing pinball was illegal up until 1976.

It Takes Two, Baby: "One witness is not enough to convict a man accused of any crime or offense he may have committed. A matter must be established by the testimony of two or three witnesses."
—*Deuteronomy 19:15*

Besides the stove, bifocals, and the Constitution, Benjamin Franklin was also known for advocating the elimination of the legal ban on bathing. Puritans had made bathing illegal on the grounds that nudity of any kind was a sin.

Thank you, Oliver Cromwell. . . . Christmas, plum pudding, and mince pie were made illegal in England in 1647.

Ten-pin bowling as we know it today was the result of skirting the laws that prohibited the original game of Nine Pins.

In the first mandate of its kind, the Massachusetts School Law made it a requirement of any town having more than fifty families to set up a school. A stiff fine of $5 was slapped on any town not obeying the law. This was in colonial America, in 1647.

Nine years earlier, in 1638, the Virginia legislature had passed a law outlawing lawyers.

two

fightin' Words

"Lawyers are jackals."

> —*Erasmus, Dutch philosopher*
> *and theologian (1466–1536)*

"Lawyers are a learned class of very ignorant men."

> —*Erasmus, Dutch philosopher*
> *and theologian (1466–1536)*

"A good lawyer is a great liar."
"A lawyer is a conscience for hire."

> —*Fyodor Dostoevsky, writer*

"Being a good robber is like being a good lawyer."

> —*Willie Sutton, bank robber*

"If laws could speak, they'd complain of the lawyers."

—George Saville, Marquess of Halifax (1633–1695)

"He is no lawyer who cannot take two sides."

—Charles Lamb, author

"If it weren't for the lawyers, we wouldn't need them."

—William Jennings Bryan, famous lawyer

"I used to be a lawyer, but now I am reformed."

—President Woodrow Wilson

"The first thing we do," says a character in the middle of *King Henry VI,* part 2, "let's kill all the lawyers."

"Lawyers, I suppose, were children once."
—*Charles Lamb, writer*

As to the lawyer, Seneca once wrote, "He lets out for hire his anger and his speech."

We don't like to bring it up, but there are some bottom-feeder sorts of lawyers for whom very interesting and descriptive names have been invented, including ambulance chaser, jackleg lawyer, latrine lawyer, pettifogger, lawmonger, and ambidexter.

"Have you noticed how much those who deal in absolutes—magistrates, policemen, priests—are generally quite humorless?"

—*Hubert Monteilhet, French author*

You may be familiar with the name for an unscrupulous lawyer, Shyster, but where did it come from? Most likely from long ago when *shy* meant "disreputable."

Dean Roscoe Pound of Harvard Law School noted that "every Utopia has been designed to dispense with lawyers."

Even Jesus found it hard to love lawyers. Luke 11:52 quotes this tirade: "Woe unto you, lawyers! For you have taken away the key of knowledge."

Poor Piggies: "Most lawyers are swine," said *San Francisco Chronicle* columnist Charles McCabe. "And not even nice swine."

"**L**aw school is the opposite of sex. Even when it's good it's lousy."

—*Unknown*

Oh, That H. L.!: "Courtroom: A place where Jesus Christ and Judas Iscariot would be equals, with the betting odds in favor of Judas," pronounced satirist H. L. Mencken.

"**L**awyers spend a great deal of their time shoveling smoke."

—*Oliver Wendell Holmes Jr., lawyer*

"What is an attorney but a college graduate who couldn't get into medical school?"

—*Major Charles Emerson Winchester,*
in the television show M*A*S*H

From the *American Legion* magazine: "The problem with lawyer jokes is that lawyers don't think they're funny, and everyone else doesn't think that they're jokes."

It's all an illusion. Magician Houdini once commented on lawyers, "They do tricks even I can't figure out."

three

Yo-Ho, Yo-Ho,
A Lawyer's Life for Me

"Lawyers must go to school for years and years, often with little sleep and with great sacrifice to their first wives."

—*Roy G. Blout Jr., humorist*

Puzzling: "If you think that you can think about a thing, inextricably attached to something else, without thinking of the thing it is attached to, then you have a legal mind," says Thomas Reed Powell, legal writer.

Thomas More is the patron saint of lawyers.

St. John's Wort is an old herbal remedy for depression. It was first discovered in the seventeenth century by lawyers.

Richard Pryor is credited with coining the term "MoFo" as a shortened version of a taboo slang term. It caused a great deal of consternation at the international law firm of Morrison & Foerster, which had been using "MoFo" as its nickname for nearly a hundred years.

"Lawyers and tarts are the two oldest professions in the world. And we always aim to please."

> —*Horace Rumpole, the fictional lawyer*
> *in the book* Rumpole of the Bailey

Aaron Burr killed Alexander Hamilton in a famous duel. Their earlier relationship planted the seed of mutual animosity: They were law partners.

"Whatever their other contributions to our society, lawyers could be an important source of protein."

> —*Caption from the late, great* Guindon *comic strip*

According to the folklore of Silesa, any child born on Christmas Day will likely become either a lawyer or a thief.

The North American black-necked stilt is also known as the "lawyer" bird because, according to the *Oxford English Dictionary,* one of its identifying features is "a large bill."

JAWS

The mechanical shark in the movie *Jaws* had the nickname "Bruce." He was named after Steven Spielberg's lawyer Bruce Ramer.

No Surprises Here: The first victim eaten by a dinosaur in the Spielberg movie *Jurassic Park* was the lawyer.

"In my youth," said his father, "I took
    to the law,
And argued each case with my wife;
And the muscular strength, which it gave
    to my jaw,
Has lasted the rest of my life."

—Lewis Carroll,
"You Are Old, Father William"

The patron saint of law schools is Raymond of Peñafort.

Graduate statistics bear out that the older you are when you graduate from law school, the more likely you are to take a job with a university rather than a job with a private firm or a corporation.

Of an estimated 25,000 law graduates in Japan who take the bar exam each year, only about 700 pass.

"In university, they don't tell you that the greater part of the law is learning to tolerate fools."

—Doris Lessing, novelist

According to a recent poll in *Bartender* magazine, lawyers tied with doctors as the worst tippers.

Deuteronomy's the specific book of the Holy Book that a wannabe Israelite law student would study before taking the bar exam. It's the Hebrew book of instruction and contains Jewish law as handed down from God to Moses.

Let's say your law firm's phone number spells something like 1-800-SUE-THEM. That's called a "numeronym."

One dreaded Mexican curse goes something like this: "May your life be filled with lawyers."

"It is the trade of lawyers to question everything, yield nothing, and talk by the hour."

—*Thomas Jefferson*

Have you heard of the "lawyer fish"? A member of the cod family, lawyer fish are found in swampy, murky regions of North America and are characterized by barbels (whiskers) on their noses and chins. If you catch one, be careful! Even while hooked they can easily wrap their bodies around your arm and squeeze it in a death-like grip . . . not unlike some of the humans who share their name.

Author Edna St. Vincent Millay clearly rather liked lawyers . . . down deep, anyway. She once said, "Lawyers are lambs in wolves' clothing."

"A FAIR FEE FOR SERVICES RENDERED

Four sheep, a hog and ten bushels of wheat settled an Iowa breach of promise suit where $25,000 damages were demanded. The lawyers got all but the hog, which died before they could drive it away."

—*Article in the* Cheyenne Leader,
January 14, 1888

four

Don't Know Much about History

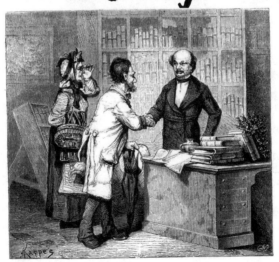

Ancient Athens chose representatives (all men) for its 500-seat lawmaking body—the Council—by lottery. Each man served for a year until the next lottery was held.

The first medical malpractice lawsuit on record—a plaintiff alleging that an inept physician maimed his hand—took place nearly 650 years ago in England.

There was a law that changed the mile officially from 5,000 feet to 5,280 feet, or exactly 8 furlongs. Queen Elizabeth I passed it in 1575, when *furlongs* actually meant something.

A fundamental part of the Constitution of South Carolina—a section on religious freedom—was drafted by noted English philosopher John Locke.

Truth as a defense against libel came after Peter Zenger attacked Governor William Cosby in 1733 of (among other things) having foul denture breath.

Early Americans

Lawyer John Adams was an American patriot who emphatically opposed the British crown. Still, his sense of justice led him to defend four British soldiers who were accused of shooting into an angry mob of American rioters during the Boston Massacre. While defending themselves against the mob, the soldiers killed four Americans. Adams managed to get two of them acquitted; the other two were convicted of manslaughter. Adams feared his actions would cost him popularity—he'd initially received threats and been met with public disapproval—but that didn't happen. Justice prevailed: In 1770, the people of Boston chose him as one of their representatives in the colonial legislature, and he was eventually elected as the United States' second president.

The two British soldiers who were convicted of manslaughter for killing four Americans were sentenced to having their thumbs branded with a hot iron. Since the twelfth century in England and from the beginning of the American court system, branding of the thumb was the common judicial sentencing for convicted men who claimed "benefit of clergy." That meant they claimed a life-changing religious conversion since their crimes were committed. This plea could only be used once by laymen. The burnt thumb would signify to any future judge and court that they'd been given the benefit of the doubt once; excuses the next time around wouldn't be heard. The practice ended in America in the 1790s.

The average age of the deputies to America's Constitutional Convention in 1787 was about forty-four. The youngest was New Jersey's Jonathan Dayton at twenty-six. The oldest was Pennsylvania's Benjamin Franklin, so infirm at eighty-one he had to be carried around in a sedan chair. Both signed the Constitution.

Only thirty-nine of the fifty-five attending delegates to the Constitutional Convention actually signed the Constitution. Fourteen had already left for home before the document was ready to be signed, and three refused to sign. Although technically absent, one of the "signatures"—John Dickinson—was forged at his request by his friend George Read.

Rhode Island didn't even send delegates to the Constitutional Convention. Furthermore, perhaps distracted by the charms of the big city (Philadelphia), nineteen delegates from other states never attended any of the convention's meetings.

Thirty-four of the delegates were lawyers. The remaining members included farmers, educators, soldiers, businessmen, financiers, physicians, and clergymen. The Constitution was drafted in about 100 working days. Jacob Shallus was the clerk who penned the Constitution after the content therein had been agreed upon. He was paid $30 for his work.

James Madison may be the "Father of the Constitution," but Benjamin Franklin was known as the "Sage of the Constitutional Convention." Thomas Jefferson—responsible for the successful adoption of the Bill of Rights—was absent at the Constitutional Convention, not because he was protesting this decisive moment in American politics but because he was serving his country as minister to France at the time.

That Noah Webster was a crack-up. When the founding fathers were wrestling with the Bill of Rights, Webster sarcastically suggested a few that didn't quite make the final cut. Here's a sampling: Guaranteed good fishing, guaranteed good weather, no restraints on sensible eating or drinking, and the right to lie on your left side or back when tired of the right side.

The first school to teach law, and only law, was in Litchfield, Connecticut. It opened its doors in 1774 and closed them for good in 1833. The college of William and Mary opened up its law professorship program—the first of its kind in the United States—in 1779.

The state of New York was the first to require motor vehicles to be licensed. This was in 1901.

Many states once mandated that margarine had to be a different color than butter. It was begun as a protection to the butter industry so consumers wouldn't mistake the products. One of the alternate colors (other than white)? Pink.

The U.S. income tax was supposed to be only a temporary money-raising solution during the Civil War. The problem came when Congress realized how much money could be gleaned this way. The U.S. Supreme Court knocked the income tax down, but Congress reinstated it in 1913 by passing the 16th Amendment.

Truth in Advertising

Before it was ruled illegal to blatantly make false claims about a product in an advertising, Grape-Nuts cereal once claimed these health benefits: "prevents appendicitis," "heals tuberculosis," "cures malaria," and most important, "tightens loose teeth."

Before false product claims in ads were made illegal, noncaffeinated Postum cornered a market by slaughtering coffee's reputation. Among other blatant lies, Postum claimed that coffee "kills your energy and reduces your working force," "pushes you into the big crowd of mongrels," contributes to "lost eyesight," "deadens whatever thoroughbred blood you may have," and thoroughly "neutralizes all your efforts to make money and fame."

The ACLU once ran a newspaper ad seeking a teacher willing to test the law about teaching evolution in the classrooms of Tennessee. This was how they found John Scopes. He answered their ad, and the rest is history.

The drink is called Kool-Aid instead of Kool-ade because back when creator

Edwin Perkins concocted his powdered drink, the FDA ruled that *ade* had to legally mean "a drink made from."

During Prohibition, information about how to homebrew alcohol was never made illegal. In fact, the U.S. Department of Agriculture distributed pamphlets on how to make alcohol from farm produce.

The National Recovery Act of 1933 called for no child labor, a 35–40 hour work week, and a minimum wage of 30 cents an hour. However, if business owners didn't comply with this law, the only penalty was a stern letter demanding that they return their Blue Eagle NRA window sign.

1941 was a pivotal year for fingerprint evidence in the United States. Although fingerprints had been used as evidence in a court of law before that point, the state always had simultaneously to submit proof that no two fingerprints were alike. The Texas Court of Criminal Appeals changed that burden of proof after undergoing a thorough examination of all of the evidence that showed that fingerprints were, indeed, unique enough to be sufficient evidence.

Opium wasn't outlawed in the United States until 1942. That same year, the Department of Agriculture stopped all aid to farmers growing poppies for the production of the drug.

Brown v. Board of Education struck down segregated schools in 1954 after an irate black father sued a school district over bad treatment of his child. Oliver Brown, the father and giant behind the landmark legal case, was a welder of boxcars.

Heads of State

If convicted, presidential killers Lee Harvey Oswald and John Wilkes Booth wouldn't have been considered "federal felons." Until after the murder of John F. Kennedy it wasn't a federal felony to kill a president, just a state felony like any other murder.

When JFK was assassinated in '63, Lyndon Baines Johnson phoned no less than three Dallas lawyers to locate a copy of the presidential Oath of Office so he could be sworn in quickly on Air Force One.

Richard Nixon was Pepsi-Cola's chief legal counsel following his first defeat in a presidential election. The company helped finance his successful bid in later years. As a matter of fact, if conspiracy theories are your bag, on November 22, 1963, the day JFK was assassinated, Nixon was in Dallas attending a Pepsi convention. He wasn't forthcoming with his whereabouts when questioned.

The Miranda behind the Miranda Rights case (1966) was a young man named Ernesto Miranda. While behind bars for stealing $8, a woman who'd been kidnapped and raped picked him out of the lineup as her attacker. The police managed to obtain a confession, but the U.S. Supreme Court tossed it out because Ernesto had not been advised of his right to not incriminate himself.

In the end, Ernesto Miranda was convicted of stealing the $8, was paroled, and later was stabbed to death in a bar.

What's the Matter with Kids

The Gault Decision in 1967 established that juveniles are entitled to due process as laid out in the Bill of Rights. This Supreme Court ruling in favor of juvenile rights is the equivalent of Miranda Rights for adults.

The Gault behind *In re Gault* (1967) was a fifteen-year-old boy named Gerald Gault. One night in 1964 he was arrested for making an indecent phone call to his neighbor. The police took him without informing his parents or allowing him to obtain a lawyer. He was then railroaded in court and sentenced to six years for his "crime," with no possibility for appeal. The U.S. Supreme Court eventually overturned that ruling.

That 25th Amendment is an important one to the second in command. Passed in 1967, it makes it possible for the vice president to take over presidential duties if the president becomes disabled. The first and only U.S. president to invoke the 25th Amendment while ill was Ronald Reagan, when he underwent surgery for colon cancer in July 1985.

It wasn't until 1989 that the Supreme Court finally ruled that the 1st Amendment included the right to burn the U.S. flag.

Both France and Russia attempted to abolish the practice of law after their revolutions.

five

Skirting the Law

Wyoming was the first state to grant women the right to vote, in 1869, when it was just a territory.

No woman could legally practice law in the United States until 1872.

Myra Colby Bradwell was the first female attorney in the United States.

The 19th Amendment in the Constitution gave American women the right to vote in 1920.

The first Westernized country to give women the legal right to vote was New Zealand in 1893. Ninety thousand women showed up at the polls. The last country was Liechtenstein in 1984.

Switzerland didn't give women the right to vote until 1971.

"Men make laws, but women make morals."

—*French proverb*

One-half: The portion of female lawyers married . . . to other lawyers.

The sale of contraceptives was finally made legal in Ireland in 1979. The use of contraceptives still goes against Roman Catholic Church law.

Despite the illiteracy rate among women in Muslim countries, Islamic law requires that both sexes be educated.

Although prostitution is not illegal there, women in Denmark are specifically forbidden by law from "walking like a prostitute."

In the Middle Ages, it was a common belief that kittens could invade a person's body and scratch them from the inside. The belief made the defense of "removing cats from the belly," a popular and winning one among women accused of having abortions.

In that spunky girl detective series about Nancy Drew, her father, Carson Drew, is a very successful criminal attorney.

Supreme Court Justice Ruth Bader Ginsberg's childhood nickname was "Kiki."

Beverly Hills socialite Sandra West provided in her will that she was to be buried "in my lace nightgown and my Ferrari, with the seat slanted comfortably." She was (and is) buried just like that . . . under pounds of concrete to prevent the theft of her very expensive car.

Most people know about Lizzie Borden, the "forty whacks," and the "not guilty" verdict in her 1897 murder trial. But did you know a warrant was issued for her arrest a second time, five years later? Not for murder, but for shoplifting. Her lawyer settled with the store owner out of court.

Law school enrollment of women has increased over the years. In 1982 the percentage of women enrollees was 33. Today women make up over 45 percent of all law school graduates.

"**S**martees" are Barbie-like dolls that are designed with specific professions. Of the first to hit the stands, the Vicky the Veterinarian doll sold like hot cakes. Not so for Ashley the Attorney—she was retired the following year. Says company president: "I don't think a lot of parents want their children to be attorneys these days."

six

Barnyard Briefs

In Connecticut, the law declares that beavers have the legal right to build dams.

Talk about Blaming the Victims: As late as 1940, a man in France was burned at the stake for bestiality. Following Old Testament precepts, so were the three cows he'd had sex with.

Centuries ago, animals were often put on trial for crimes ranging from witchcraft to theft to murder. Throughout history, the animal that's been prosecuted most in court is the pig.

A Dog's Life

Contrary to what's been reported in many sources, there is no ban on dogs in Iceland. Icelandic law states that dogs should have space to run free in the countryside. For this reason within the populated city limits of the capital, Reykjavik, there are strict limitations on owning a pet.

Plato believed a dog would be a good addition to any courtroom because, he reasoned, dogs can tell when someone's lying.

If a bloodhound has detected criminal evidence in a case, its "testimony" (the evidence that was sniffed out . . . or not) is admissible in a court of law.

A dog in Virginia can be detained and killed for "barking criminally."

☜ ☞

In 1963 Tripoli, the courts sentenced seventy-five convicted banknote smugglers to death at one time. They were all pigeons.

Speaking of Barnyard Animal Behavior: The Iowa state legislature officially declared Kansas' state flower—the sun flower—a noxious weed. In retaliation, Kansas declared the Iowa state bird— the Easter Goldfinch—an official public nuisance.

Cat and Mouse

Ye Olde Spanish Proverb: "It's better to be a mouse in the mouth of a cat than a man in the hands of a lawyer."

Cats were considered holy in ancient Egypt, and it was against the law to export them. As a result, cat smuggling was a huge business.

Japanese lawmakers have been known, on occasion, to fist fight. Alabama lawmakers make barnyard animal noises, while British lawmakers heckle. It's nothing new: The old Roman Senate's lawmakers used to make raspberry sounds to jeer at each other while in session.

The only known criminal hanging of an elephant took place in Erwin, Tennessee, on September 13, 1916. The convict's name was Five-Ton Mary, and she had killed a keeper.

Let the Lawyer Speak: From one official court transcript comes this gem: The judge turns to the defendant, "The charge here is theft of frozen chickens. Are you the defendant, sir?" "No," replied the defendant, "I'm the guy who stole the chickens."

You cannot legally have a gerbil as a pet in California. If they get loose, they thrive, multiply, and devastate crops.

In 1840s Slavonia a pig once chewed off a little girl's ear. In court the owner of the pig was forced to provide for the girl's dowry.

It's against the law to offer an animal a cigar in Zion, Illinois . . . but no mention is made of cigarettes, pipes, or chewing gum.

It's illegal in Pacific Grove, California, to kill or threaten a butterfly.

seven

It's the Law!

"The more numerous the laws, the more corrupt the state."

—*Tacitus, Roman writer (A.D. 56–120)*

Every year, Americans are saddled with more than 150,000 new laws and 2 million regulations.

Most people are familiar with the laws in Singapore that severely punish graffiti and chewing gum in public places. But did you know that it's also illegal to overwater your plants, fail to flush your toilet, or pee in an elevator?

At one time, Japanese laws regulated what colors were acceptable for office equipment. Beige was one of those colors. When product designer Jerry Manock was deciding on a color for the Apple II in the late 1970s, the Japanese laws factored into his decision to choose beige. Aside from wanting to sell Apples in Japan, he also found that the color had the added benefit of hiding dust well.

Good News! "Do Not Remove Under Penalty of Law" tags on mattresses, pillows, and furniture can be removed without fear once you bring them home. The tags are there for the protection of the customer. It seems there was a time, not so long ago, when furniture manufacturers were sometimes known to make their wares from lesser quality and cheaper materials than they would claim. The tags are officially informing buyers of the materials in the furniture.

The law is . . .

"a bum profession."
>—*Clarence Darrow Scopes, trial lawyer*

"a dull dog."
>—*Charles Dickens, author*

"a humbug."
>—*Henry David Thoreau, author*

"a heathen word for power."
>—*Daniel Defoe, author*

"a hard, queer thing I do not understand."
>—*Chief Poundmaker (Cree Indian)*

"valuable not because it is law, but because there is right in it."
>—*Reverend Henry Ward Beecher*

"a causeway upon which so long as he keeps to it a citizen may walk safely."
>—*Robert Bolt, screenwriter*

"neither a cause, nor a reason, nor a power, nor a coercive force. It is nothing but a general formula; a statistical table."

—Florence Nightingale, nurse

"stable and yet it must not stand still."

*—Roscoe Pound, American jurist
and author*

"made to take care o' raskills."

—George Eliot, author

New Jersey and Oregon both have laws that prohibit self-service pumping of gasoline.

"Bad laws are the worst sort of tyranny."

*—Edmund Burke, political philosopher
(1729–1797)*

Appellation d'Origin Controlee is a mouthful. Simply put, it's the French legal code for top-of-the-line wines coming from France. It translates to "name of controlled origin" and is often written as AOC. In Italian, a similar class of wine is called *denominazione di origine controllata* (DOC). The Germans say *qualitatswein mit pradikat* (QmP) and the Spanish *denominacion de origen calificada* (DOC). American wines have no legal wine classification like this (thank God).

In Shakespeare's *King Henry VIII*, Lord Chamberlain placed a great deal of faith in the legal process, rather than kicking a man when he's down:

Press not a falling man too far! 'tis virtue:
His faults lie open to the laws; let them,
Not you, correct him.

"Where law ends, tyranny begins."
   —William Pitt, prime minister of England
                        (1759–1806)

The Nürnberg Laws were the 1935 Nazi edicts that took away citizenship and other rights of all German-born Jews. In a little bit of poetic justice, after the war, the city of Nürnberg was a site for the trials of accused German war criminals.

"How noble the law, in its majestic equal-
   ity, that both the rich and poor are equally

prohibited from peeing in the streets, sleeping under bridges, and stealing bread!"

—*Anatole France, French novelist*

Chinese philosopher Lao-tzu believed one thing often led to another. "The more laws, the more thieves," he once wrote.

In order to impeach a Supreme Court justice, the Constitution dictates that the Impeachment Resolution must come from the House, while the official trial is to be overseen by the Senate and "all civil Officers," which includes the remaining Supreme Court justices.

The U.S. Constitution, in all of its pages, mentions just one specific crime: treason.

You can't be convicted of treason against the United States without two separate witnesses' testimony reporting the exact same and specific illegal act. Or unless you confess it yourself in court.

Under the law, you need at least three persons to constitute a "riot."

The ancient Roman philosopher, politician, and lawyer Marcus Tullius Cicero had a lot of observations. Here's one meandering on law: "Laws are dumb in time of war."

The British Constitution, in contrast to the American version, can be changed overnight by an act of Parliament. The constitution is considered a "flexible" document and is in unwritten form. As a lecturer in constitutional law liked to put it to his students, "A slight problem that you are going to have in studying the British Constitution is that Britain doesn't have a constitution per se."

Common law—that which British and U.S. law is based upon—is also known as "unwritten law" because it doesn't come from one, single source but rather from centuries of tradition and common use. Louisiana is the only state in the union that bases its laws not on English common law but on French civil law.

"The common law itself is nothing else but reason."

—*Sir Edward Coke, British attorney general (1552–1634)*

The hierarchy of law in the United States is the Constitution, followed by treaties with foreign powers and acts of Congress, state constitutions, state statutory law, and, finally, the common law.

The Supreme Court has declared that the Constitution absolutely does not exclude convicted felons from the voting process. The decision to strip felons of their right to vote is purely a state one.

In Maine, buildings made of round logs are tax-exempt.

Under the United States Uniform Code of Military Justice, soldiers or sailors posing naked commit a criminal offense.

Until 1986, each state in the United States decided what their minimum drinking age would be. That year saw the introduction of the National Minimum Drinking Age Act, which pretty much forced all states to adopt the age of twenty-one.

Although you must be twenty-one in the United States to *purchase* alcoholic beverages, in at least nineteen states it's not specifically against the law to *consume* alcohol if you're under twenty-one.

According to the International Center for Alcohol Policies, the only other countries besides the United States that have a minimum drinking age law of twenty-one are South Korea, Malaysia, and the Ukraine.

"There are not enough jails, not enough policemen, not enough courts to enforce a law not supported by the people."
—*Vice President Hubert H. Humphrey*

Sobriety's a legal necessity when driving a car, but what about when riding a horse? A horse, too, says the law. It's defined as a vehicle. Passenger—and horse—must be sober.

Members of England's House of Lords are not allowed to vote in general elections. Members of British royal family are not allowed to vote at all.

You can copyright a journal that was written in the past twenty years. You can copyright your grocery list presented as a poem. You can copyright a song lyric inspired by an instrumental work or a limerick about your lawyer. What *can't* you copyright? The title of your book.

Not true that the German Autobahn doesn't have a speed limit: it's 81 mph (130 kph) in some of the more accident-prone places.

"The law is reason free from passion."
—*Aristotle, Greek philosopher (384–322 B.C.)*

"Law guards us from all evils but itself."
—*Henry Fielding, English judge and playwright (1707–1754)*

In order to maintain your U.S. citizenship, there are just a few things you can't do under the law: You can't serve in another country's army or vote in another country's

election. You mustn't be convicted of treason. And if you renounce your citizenship
formally, you will also lose it.

A silicon chip design—as with all patents
on designs—is protected by law for only
fourteen years, instead of the standard
seventeen for other types of patents.

Georgia law specifically forbids "selling
a minor under age 12 . . . to rope or wire
walk, beg, be a gymnast, contortionist,
circus rider, acrobat or clown."

David Dinkins, former mayor of New York
City, on failing to pay his taxes, came up
with this little legalistic gem: "I haven't

committed a crime. What I did was fail to comply with the law."

He's not said much since, but Clarence Thomas once said, "Government cannot make us equal: It can only recognize, respect, and protect us as equal before the law."

By law, Atlantic City, New Jersey, slot machines must pay out 83 percent of their take.

Canada's courtroom judges cannot vote in general elections.

"We are slaves of the law in order that we may be able to be free."

—*Marcus Tullius Cicero*

Shoot First; Ask Questions Later: "Make My Day" is the slang name for the Colorado law that allows for a person to shoot an intruder if the shooter believes he's in danger.

An "Enoch Arden law" allows for remarriage after a spouse's long, unexplained absence. Who or what was Enoch Arden? He was a fictitious lost-at-sea character from a poem by Alfred, Lord Tennyson.

Speaking of literary laws, Rudyard Kipling's *Law of the Jungle* dictated that "the strength of the pack is the wolf, and the strength of the wolf is the pack."

If the 1996 Communications Decency Act had become law, Congress could have been fined $250,000 for posting Ken Starr's sexually explicit report online.

Martin Luther King Jr. had this to say about "that old law about 'an eye for an eye'": "It leaves everyone blind."

"**I**f a man were permitted to write the songs, he need not care who should make the laws of a nation."

—*Andrew Fletcher, Scottish nationalist*
(1655–1716)

Noise Pollution: An old law still in effect requires that a driver honk the horn at every intersection in Caracas, Venezuela.

Said author Francis Bacon (1561–1626): "The laws are like cobwebs: the small flies get caught and the great break through."

According to the FDA's *Food Defect Action Levels Handbook,* a normal-sized jar of peanut butter is legally allowed to contain up to 210 insect fragments and 7 whole rodent hairs before it's officially deemed unsanitary.

"Laws are like sausages. It's better not to see them being made."
—*German Chancellor Otto von Bismarck (1815–1898)*

eight

Larger
than Life

Alan Dershowitz became a full professor at Harvard Law School at the age of twenty-eight, making him the youngest professor in the school's history. Dershowitz's client list reads something like a Who's Who of the rich and famous. Here are a few: Jim Bakker, John DeLorean, Patty Hearst, Leona Helmsley, Michael Milken, Mike Tyson, and Clause von Bulow.

Richard Nixon's first legal case was bungled so badly, it cost his firm thousands of dollars. Because it looked as though he had unethically tried to gain financially from the case, the judge issued this serious warning to him: "Mr. Nixon, I have serious doubts whether you have the ethical qualifications to practice law in the state of California. I am seriously thinking about turning this matter over to the Bar Association." After being slapped down in the first legal trial of his career, Richard Nixon seriously and sulkily thought of leaving the United States and setting up a law practice in Havana, Cuba. He went so far as to travel there and check out the opportunities.

The Marquess of Queensbury is best known for formulating modern boxing rules; however, it also should be remembered he was the man behind the sensational lawsuit that brought down Oscar Wilde for having a homosexual relationship with the Marquess' son.

The infamous Sir Henry Morgan, known for his pillaging of the Spanish Main, sued for libel when he was called a pirate in print. Because his piracy was endorsed by the government (he was a "privateer," after all), the London jury awarded him 200 pounds for defamation of character.

One man who must have hated Henry Ford was a sharp Philadelphia lawyer named George B. Selden. Seeing where auto manufacturers were headed, the lawyer patented a very basic blueprint of a simple motor car before anybody else did. He then used that patent to bully payment from manufacturers of any and all automobiles. By 1895 automobile manufacturers were paying Selden $5 for every car produced. But in 1911 Ford refused and sued, and the patent was voided.

Student
Radical

Vladimir Lenin was tossed out of Kazan University Law School only three months into his studies. The reason for his expulsion? He was caught demonstrating for freedom and accused of being a student radical.

Lenin was eventually accepted into St. Petersburg University. He received a law degree in 1891 and joined a law firm in the Russian city of Samara.

☞ ☜

Pope Saint Gregory the Great was a Roman lawyer and administrator.

Was "Rushmore" the guy who discovered or carved the mountain? No, he was a lawyer. In 1885 a New York attorney named Charles Rushmore was riding through the area and asked the name of the mountain. His guide teased the city slicker: "Hell, it never had a name but from now on we'll call the damned thing Rushmore." Strangely enough, the name stuck. The lawyer Rushmore, by the way, never abandoned his rocky namesake—he was one of the first to donate a large sum of money toward carving the mountainside.

There's a Web site that sells movie stars' last wills and testaments. You can pick up copies of James Dean's and Frank Sinatra's for $12.99. If your budget can't accommodate that, there's always Judy Garland's or John Wayne's, which sell for a mere $9.99. *www.hollywoodwebshop.com/gifts/wills.shtml*

A lot of people know that Abe Lincoln was a lawyer back in Illinois before being elected president, but most people don't know that he was also a licensed bartender. He had to be, because he was co-owner of a saloon in Springfield, Illinois, called Berry & Lincoln.

Forget Johnny Cochran. Clarence Darrow was the defense lawyer for three of the "Trials of the Century:" The 1924 Leopold-Loeb murder trial, in which two teens were tried for murdering a third just for "kicks"; the Scopes Trial, in which he defended the teaching of evolution; and the Big Bill Haywood Trial, in which labor organizer Haywood was acquitted of murdering a former governor of Idaho.

Joseph Ritson, the vegetarian atheist who in 1795 resurrected the mostly forgotten Robin Hood story, despised attorneys. He argued that the guilty didn't deserve a lawyer's representation and the innocent by definition didn't need it.

Ironically, conservative Supreme Court Chief Justice William Rehnquist not only shares a birthday with former Democratic president Jimmy Carter, but the actual year, as well: October 1, 1924. That makes them Libras, and according to the Chinese Zodiac, they're both Rats.

Famous lawyer Daniel Webster never attended law school.

Scopes Trial defender Clarence Darrow was a law school dropout. He went one year, then dropped out to study the law on his own.

Esteemed lawyers Abraham Lincoln and Stephen Douglas were once rivals over Mary Todd's affections (Lincoln won), but more important, they argued continuously over legal and political issues. Neither one of them ever attended a law school of any kind.

In case you were wondering, Pliny the Elder was the scientist. It was his nephew and adopted son, Pliny the Younger, who was the lawyer.

Legendary lawman Wyatt Earp was kicked out of the entire state of California for horse thievery.

Clarence Darrow was accused of attempting to bribe two jurors during a trial where two brothers were charged with blowing up the *Los Angeles Times* building. Although he was technically acquitted, many legal historians believe he was actually guilty of bribery.

Although now famous as a philosopher and author (some say he even wrote Shakespeare's plays), Francis Bacon was infamous in his day. While serving as England's lord chancellor, he was removed from office for accepting a litigant's bribe.

> **"There is no worse torture
> than that of laws."**
>
> —*Francis Bacon, philosopher (1561–1626)*

nine

Judge Not, Lest Ye Be Judged

"Judges, like the criminal classes, have their lighter moments."

— *Oscar Wilde, playwright*

When judges in ancient China heard evidence, they wore spectacles of smoke-colored quartz to mask their reactions.

The chief justice is the only Supreme Court justice mentioned specifically in the Constitution.

The salary for the chief justice of the Supreme Court is $181,400 per year. Associate justices make about $173,600.

"A lifetime of law alone turns judges into dull, dry husks."

—*Judge William O. Douglas*

The U.S. Supreme Court justices meet in a building inscribed simply with "Equal Justice under Law."

Supreme Court Justice Roger B. Taney (1836–1864) was the first justice to wear trousers beneath his judicial robes. Prior to that point, justices sported knee breeches.

The only Supreme Court justice never to have held a public office prior to his appointment was Joseph P. Bradley (1870–1892).

In 1949 Sherman "Shay" Minton became the last Supreme Court justice to use the spittoon that was provided for the justices behind the bench. This habit terribly upset fellow Justice Harold Burton, who had the misfortune of sitting next to Minton on the bench. Burton was presumably relieved when Minton retired seven years later.

You've heard of federal Judge Learned Hand, but did you know that his first name was actually Billings? "Learned" was his middle name, and he liked it better.

Supreme Court Justice Joseph Story, appointed in 1811, published his own book of poetry at age twenty-six before going into law. While he served on the bench, he also served as a bank president.

Justice Joseph Story was the youngest Supreme Court justice in history. He was appointed to the bench at the age of thirty-two. He served for thirty-four years and is considered the court's greatest legal scholar.

1886 was the first year that Congress provided a budget for Supreme Court justices to hire law clerks to assist them in their duties. In that day it was a grand total of $1,600 for one year's salary (the equivalent of about $31,000 today). Today a Supreme Court law clerk makes, on average, around $44,000 a year.

Supreme Court Justice Antonin Scalia was once an actor at the Georgetown Theatre.

Political Stage Fellows: In 1994 Justices Ruth Ginsburg and Antonin Scalia appeared in a Washington Opera performance of Richard Strauss' *Ariadne auf Naxos.* They appeared together as extras, donning white wigs and eighteenth-century dress.

Chief Justice John Marshall, who served from 1801 to 1835, is ranked at the top of every list of great Supreme Court justices. He is the longest serving Supreme Court chief justice in the history of the Supreme Court.

Justice Horace Lurton is the oldest Supreme Court justice ever appointed. He was ready to turn sixty-six when President William H. Taft placed him on the bench in 1909.

Oliver Wendell Holmes was the oldest Supreme Court justice to sit on the bench. He was ninety years old when he retired in 1932.

Theodore Roosevelt was once furious with Oliver Wendell Holmes for writing a dissenting opinion on an antitrust case. Roosevelt fired off a scathing letter that included this memorable insult: " I've seen more backbone in a banana!"

That's nothing. President Truman appointed Justice Tom Clark, then remarked later that Clark was "the dumbest man . . . I've ever run across." Except maybe presidents . . .

"There are no more reactionary people than judges."

—*V. I. Lenin*

Supreme Court Justice John Jay never attended law school.

Supreme Court Chief Justices John Marshall, Roger Taney, and Salmon P. Chase also never went to law school.

Chief Justice Earl Warren always read the sports page of the newspaper before any of the other sections. Why? Warren said it was because "the sports section records people's accomplishments. The front page is nothing but men's failures."

Chief Justice William Rehnquist graduated at the top of his 1950 class from Stanford Law School. Justice Sandra Day O'Connor graduated third in the same class.

Supreme Court Justice Felix Frankfurter once wisely cracked, "To some lawyers all facts are created equal."

"A judge is a law student who marks his own papers."

—*H. L. Mencken*

The bestselling adult Halloween mask in the United States in 1995 was a Judge Ito mask.

ten

Courtside Seats

"A jury is 12 persons deciding who has the better lawyer."

—*Robert Frost, poet*

In most places in America, lawyers, physicians, members of the clergy, and police officers are exempt from jury duty.

In 1971 a Pennsylvania man sued Satan and his minions for putting obstacles in his path and causing his downfall. The case was, not surprisingly, thrown out of court. The grounds? The defendant did not reside in the state.

In a 1986 Illinois murder trial, the defendant went berserk, punching his lawyer and the judge before being subdued by court personnel. After his conviction, he appealed on the grounds that the attack had prejudiced the judge against him.

Advises Cicero, well trained in ancient Roman law: "When you have no case, abuse the plaintiff."

The Road to Ruin: More than half of the time spent in all American courts combined is devoted to cases involving automobiles.

"When you go into court you are putting your fate into the hands of twelve people who weren't smart enough to get out of jury duty."

—*Norm Crosby, comedian*

In ancient Babylon, if you gave false testimony, you were killed.

Trial by jury hasn't gone without its share of criticisms, the first of which is reasonable doubt that individuals are capable of judging outside their own popular views. Mark Twain, never afraid to speak his mind, once said, "The jury system puts a ban upon intelligence and honesty, and a premium upon ignorance, stupidity, and perjury."

Before there were juries, Europeans went to trial in one of three ways: *Compurgation,* when an accused swore his innocence and had others swear to it as well, presenting a full defense for himself. In an *ordeal* the accused was put through physical rigors (a hot poker in the hand, dunking, being pressed by stones)—he was "innocent" if he didn't die. Finally, in *trial by combat* the parties in dispute physically fought— whoever survived (or fared the best) was the "winner."

During trial by combat a contestant could hire someone to fight in his place. Often-times these individuals were trained and made a living by being hired as surrogates in these sometimes lethal judicial battles.

Here's a double-edged Gypsy curse: "May you have a lawsuit in which you are right."

The TV lawyer who won the highest percentage of cases is Perry Mason, beating out Rumpole Bailey, Ben Matlock, Allie McBeal, and the rest. Mason lost just one case throughout his TV career: "The Case of the Deadly Verdict."

Legally, juries can be hung, but not prisoners. They're *hanged*.

Famous free-speech judge Learned Hand once warned, "Dread a lawsuit beyond anything short of sickness and death."

A brief rundown of the O. J. Simpson murder trial:

- The jurors on the case were sequestered for 266 days.

- The average age of the jurors was forty-three.

- Ten jurors were dismissed throughout the course of the trial.

- Eleven defense attorneys and nine prosecution lawyers worked during the trial.

- Judge Ito pulled the plug on the television feed twice.

- The estimated cost of the trial, minus defense costs, was about $9 million—billed to Los Angeles County.

- Each juror earned $5 per day, totaling $1,330 for each person.

- The official court transcript was more than 50,000 pages.

- There were 250 separate phone lines installed in the press room.

- The courtroom seated only eighty people.

- Fines imposed during the trial totaled $5,650. The prosecution had to pay $850, other individuals racked up $1,800, and the defense was slapped with fines of $3,000.

In the 1700s juries were not allowed to eat or drink until they arrived at a verdict. The situation led poet Alexander Pope to write this protest couplet:

Hungry judges soon the sentence sign
And wretches hang that jury-men may dine.

Creepy Conviction: Archbishop of Canterbury Thomas à Becket was still a potent martyr against the English throne 350 years after his death. Henry VIII tried to decrease his power by putting Becket's bones through a trial and then burning them.

An old Chinese proverb compares going to court with "losing a cow for the sake of a cat."

Almost all of the police and magistrate courts in the United States are not courts of record, meaning that details of the court proceedings are not kept.

The number of civil cases that come to trial are few: Only about 3 percent are settled by jury or judge.

"The plaintiff and the defendant in an action at law, are like two men ducking their heads in a bucket, and daring each other to remain longest under water."

—*Samuel Johnson*

1996 was the first year that saw U.S. courts—both state and federal—convict more than 1 million adults as felons.

On average, about one-fourth of all felony defendants in state courts around the United States are charged with a violent offense—usually simple assault.

eleven

Lawspeak

"**O**nly lawyers can write 10,000 words and call it a 'brief.'"

—*Franz Kafka, author*

The term "red tape" comes from the old practice of using red binding around official documentation—particularly government and legal documentation. This practice dates back almost 500 years.

Although it sounds like a fruity wine sauce, *jus sanguinis* is the Latin term for children inheriting their parents' citizenship.

It might go well as a seafood dish served with *jus sanguinis,* but *lapsus calami* means "a slip of the pen" in legalese.

Every time the Supreme Court justices enter the Court, the marshal recites these words: "The Honorable, the Chief Justice, and the Associate Justices of the Supreme Court of the United States. Oyez Oyez Oyez. All persons having business before the Honorable, the Supreme Court of the United States, are admonished to draw near and give their attention, for Court is now sitting. God save the United States and this honorable Court."

Oh yeah! *Oyez* can be pronounced "o-yay" or "o-yez" or "o-yes." It is shouted three times in succession when opening a court of law. *Oyez* comes from the Latin plural *audire,* meaning "to hear." The Anglo-Normans passed this on to the England's court system as *oyer.* It emerged in Middle

English as *oyez* and has remained unchanged ever since. It's a reminder that until the 1700s English was not the language used in a British court of law. Thanks to the Norman Conquest, "Law French" was the language of the official class in England.

It doesn't make sense, but in lawyerspeak "lapse statute," "antilapse statute," and "nonlapse statute" mean essentially the same thing.

Satirist Ambrose Bierce defined *litigation* as "a machine which you go into as a pig and come out as a sausage."

Legal Talk: *Habeus corpus* translates from Latin as "you may have the body." It's a phrase worth remembering in case you're anticipating an intimate moment with a law clerk.

It's Nothing Personal: In England, a verdict of *Ignoramus* means the evidence was not sufficient to convict. From the Latin, it translates to "We do not know," not "You're a moron."

Where the word *testimony* comes from: In Roman times, men put a hand on their testes when swearing an oath.

Mutatis mutandis is not the latest Disney theme song. It's a wonderful Latin phrase legally meaning "Certain changes must be taken into account."

If your girlfriend was named "Nulla Bona," you could reasonably expect that she's not got much going for her. In Latin the legal phrase translates to "no goods."

Liticaphobia is the word for "fear of law-suits."

Someone who is guilty of a tort is called a "tort-feasor."

Scot, from the Old Norse by way of Middle English, meant "tax" or "levy." To go *scot free,* therefore, means you "get away without paying."

Idiot is a Greek legal term. It meant "Those who do not vote."

The initials are confusing to lay people and even some attorneys: Until about the late '60s, LL.B—*Latin Legum Baccalaureus*—meant a person who held a bachelor of law degree. After 1970, J.D.—*Juris Doctor*—became the initials of choice to denote a basic law degree. LL.M. is used by those who've obtained a master's in law, and LL.D. represents doctors of law and is usually an honorary degree.

In old legal lingo, "in cold blood" specifically meant "premeditated"—in other words, not "in the heat of the moment."

In legal documentation the term "infant" can refer to anyone under the age of eighteen.

Those City Folk: *In pais* means something that takes place outside court proceedings. It literally means "in the country."

Despite the sound of it, "sexual commerce" is not necessarily illegal. The term is a legalism having to do with cohabiting without marriage.

An *ipse dixit* is a dogmatic statement un-supported by fact. What does the phrase mean literally? "He himself said it."

"The trouble with lawyers is that they are insufferable word stretchers."

—*Nero Wolfe, fictitious detective*

State Security Laws—laws that protect against fraudulent sales and financial trans-actions—are also known as Blue Sky Laws. The term may have come from a judge's ruling in the late 1800s about an IPO, claiming the company had as much market value as a piece of blue sky.

Lese majesty: "By his Majesty's authority," maybe? Nah, it's just another term for "treason."

The "by" in *bylaws* actually comes from the Norse, meaning "town."

You're familiar with the phrase "Possession is nine-tenths of the law"? What about "Possession is nine points of the law"? They're both the same thing, just different ways of saying it. The law is in your favor if you have an item (or property, as is usually the case) in your possession. A legal claim doesn't hold as much weight without possession.

No, *causa mortis* isn't a really bad Mexican restaurant. It's Latin legalese, generally meaning "something done in contemplation of one's own death."

Show us yours! Let's say in contractual matters you're careful to dot every *i* and *j*. You should know what that little dot is called: It's a tittle.

Ad hoc literally translates to "to this."

Legal Pairings: "Assault" and "battery" do not mean the same thing within the law. Neither do "aid" and "abet," "new" and "novel," or "premeditation" and "malice aforethought."

However, the words in the pairs "null and void," "free and clear," "acknowledge and confess," "goods and chattels," and "part and parcel" both mean the same thing legally.

According to the Supreme Court, the Great Lakes are classified for shipping the same as other large bodies of water: as high seas.

Beautiful corpse? The Latin legal term *corpus delicti* literally translates to "the body of a crime."

An inheritance more burdensome than profitable is called in legalese *damnosa hereditas.*

What does *damnum sine injuria* mean? It's not what an ancient Roman would yell if he accidentally hit a billboard; it means "loss without injury."

In England the difference between *barristers* and *solicitors* is this: Solicitors generally will work within a legal practice, whereas barristers will not; solicitors' work is primarily giving clients legal advice in office, whereas barristers' work is done within the courtroom. Today these defining lines are more blurred than they've been in the past, as some solicitors now work in court.

When a well-known British actress, notorious for her love affairs, broke her leg, Dorothy Parker remarked, "She must have done it sliding down a barrister."

twelve

Breaking Up
Is Hard
to Do

In the early twentieth century, a vending machine in Corinne, Utah, provided ready-made divorce papers. Residents would drop in ten quarters, fill out the forms, and take them to a local law firm for final action.

Think of the Legal Fees: As of 1957, an American woman, Beverly Nina Avery, had been married sixteen times! She twice married and divorced two of the same men. James Williams of Iowa brightened his lawyer's lifetime by also marrying and divorcing sixteen times, four of those times to the same woman.

Yeah, they both mean "remarriage after a divorce," but which legal term sounds like you're having more fun: *digamy* or *deuterogamy*?

The ancient Hittites had an interesting divorce settlement for broken marriages that involved a free man and slave woman. The man would gain custody of all the children, save one. No exceptions. If the wife were free and the man a slave, the wife won custody of all the children.

If two Hittite slaves were divorcing, custody of all the children, except one, went to the wife.

In Rome in the second century B.C. a woman could be divorced or even killed with impunity by her husband if he caught her drinking wine.

Muslim men wishing to divorce their wives need no judge or lawyer. According to law, one simply assembles two witnesses and in front of these he tells his wife, "I divorce thee." That's it.

By law a Muslim man gets custody of his children after divorce because they're his property.

As soon as a Muslim man divorces his wife, he is free to remarry. His wife must wait three months to determine if she is pregnant. If not, she may remarry at this time; if so, she must bear and raise the child to adulthood before remarrying.

When traditional Eskimos divorce, no lawyers get involved if the couples have no children. The dissatisfied partner moves out of the house—oftentimes in with someone else—and life goes on.

An Australian aborigine woman tradition- ally begins her divorce proceedings by eloping with another man. Otherwise, she has to somehow convince her husband, who usually has many wives, to give her away to another man or willingly divorce her.

If a Chinese marriage ended in ancient times, it was often with the official reason of "incompatibility"; however, this was only possible if the wife's family agreed to take her back.

In ancient China a husband needed only behave reprehensibly and have his own parents' approval to legally divorce his wife. However, by law and custom, if his parents had passed away and his wife had mourned their passing, he was as good as stuck in the marriage for the rest of his life.

Henry VIII irrevocably changed the ecclesiastical courts of England and established the Church of England because he wanted to marry and divorce whom he wished. He finagled the illegal marriage to his brother's widow Catherine by special dispensation from the Church. He later cut all ties with the Roman Catholic Church in order to divorce her and marry Anne Boleyn.

Napoleon Bonaparte acted as his own lawyer, judge, and jury when he granted himself an annulment from his long-term wife, Josephine, on the grounds she was sterile. When it was pointed out that she had two children from a previous marriage, Napoleon waved his hand, proclaiming he was an emperor first, not a biologist.

Prenups are now as common as marriage licenses, but a new trend sees many couples drawing up postnuptials—legal and binding agreements between married couples over property and money that are made after marriage. Many states aren't supportive of this latest craze, however. Minnesota, for instance, has declared that nuptial agreements are legal if and only if each member of the couple is worth more than $1.2 million. That narrows the field.

Prenups were commonplace in medieval Iceland. Usually prenuptial agreements governed who got what and who would hold titles following death or abandonment. One example of this was a notorious Norse queen, Queen Gunnhildr (a.k.a. "mother of kings"), who held power through her widowhood and her sons, thanks to a premarital agreement.

"**P**aying alimony is like feeding hay to a dead horse."

—*Groucho Marx, actor/comedian*

Actor John Barrymore once quipped, "You never realize how short a month is until you pay alimony."

Most notably, writer P. G. Wodehouse had this to say on alimony: "Judges, as a class, display, in the matter of arranging alimony, that reckless generosity which is found only in men who are giving away someone else's cash."

Ronald and Bonnette Askew of California had been married for more than fifteen years when she left him in 1991, explaining she'd never been sexually attracted to him. Ronald sued her for fraud. He won and, shockingly, was awarded $242,000.

Eighty-five percent of all divorced people get married again within five years. Only 40 percent of those marriages last.

The biggest divorce settlement on record occurred when Saudi arms dealer Adnan Khashoggi split with his wife Soraya in 1982. She got a whopping $950 million.

In the Malabar region of India, a woman divorces her husband by leaving his shoes outside the door.

By old Anglo-Saxon law, a wife who was too passionate could be divorced by her husband.

Laughter must be the best medicine: The show biz group with the lowest divorce rate is comedians.

thirteen

I Fought the Law
and the Law Won

Despite what you may have heard, Socrates didn't get the death penalty when he was convicted of "denying the gods and corrupting youth." He received the death penalty for his impudence in refusing to show contrition or plead for mercy before the 281 (of 501) freemen jury who had found him guilty of the first charges.

Ancient Nesilim (Hittite) law required not an eye for an eye but a pound of silver for blinding a sighted man. That equaled almost 55 shekels. The fine was eventually knocked down to only 20 half-shekels— not even the cost of an ox at the time.

According to ancient Hittite law, knocking out a man's teeth brought the same settlement as blinding him—20 half-shekels.

Hittite laws regarding sex were a little confusing. For instance, you could have sex with any slave or free woman and there was no punishment, unless she was your mother, daughter, stepdaughter, mother-in-law, or your brother's wife. Those brought the death penalty. Having sex with a horse or a mule was okay, but cows, oxen, pigs, sheep, and dogs would get you death.

According to Hittite law, if you burned your neighbor's house down you were required to rebuild the house. However, anything inside the house, "be it a man, an ox, or a sheep that perishes, nothing of these he need compensate."

Product Liability in Ancient Babylon: If a house was built in a faulty way and fell on its owner, the builder was slain. If the owner's son was killed in the falling house, the builder's son was slain.

If an accused Babylonian wanted to prove his innocence, his best shot was to throw himself in the Euphrates River. If the gods pushed him back ashore, he was legally declared innocent.

In ancient Babylon, if a robber broke a hole in a house and was caught, the court put him to death at the site of the hole and buried him there.

The biblical punishment for adultery was stoning.

Beheading was even more gruesome than most people would ever imagine. An executioner often missed chopping the head off cleanly the first time, leaving the victim bleeding and howling in great pain while he tried again (and sometimes again and again) to get it right. Some condemned prisoners tipped the executioner before kneeling at the block to encourage him to sharpen his blade, aim true, and make death as quick and painless as possible.

In the 1770s, bleeding-heart humanitarian Dr. Joseph Guillotin successfully lobbied the French government to adopt a "humane" method of executing criminals. It was because of this lobbying that the machine was given his name—he didn't invent it.

According to the charts in a book called *The Business Side of Hanging,* the proper drop distance when hanging a 140-pound prisoner was exactly 9 feet, 4 inches. This book was required reading for hangmen because accurately balancing the length of the rope with their victims' weight was a source of acute professional pride. Too little drop force and the prisoner flopped like a mackerel through an agonizingly slow strangulation; too much and his head could get lopped clean off.

In Puritan times in New Haven, Connecticut, the maximum penalty for young people who cursed their parents was death. Shunning, expulsion from the community, and being locked up in stocks were lesser punishments for this crime.

In the old days of tarring and feathering miscreants, the preferred combination was pine tar and goose feathers.

In 1844 a man by the name of Jonathan Walker was convicted of trying to help slaves escape. The letters *SS* were branded onto his right palm, indicting Walker as a "slave stealer." He was the last American to be branded as punishment for a crime.

The Italian thief who stole the *Mona Lisa* from the French Louvre in 1911 was caught while trying to sell it for $95,000. However, he got off pretty lightly. During his trial he told the Florentine jury that the whole fiasco was simply an act of patriotism. They bought his argument and sentenced him only to one year and fifteen days.

The longest sentence ever given to a prisoner is most likely 30,000 years, given in 1999 to Charles Scott Robinson of Oklahoma City for rape.

The drunk tank in Japanese police stations is nobly called the "Tiger Box."

The punishment for minor offenses in Yemen is leg irons. It's pretty universal there: The punishment's the same for juveniles and adults.

The maximum federal penalty for "whale harassment" is a $10,000 fine.

From a January 21, 1999, Knight-Ridder news dispatch: "The federal death penalty, reinstated by the Senate in the recent crime bill, was reserved for certain violent crimes like assassinating the President, hijacking an airplane, and murdering a government poultry inspector."

Currently thirty-nine states in the United States make use of the death penalty for treason and murder. The most popular method is lethal injection, but other methods include electrocution, gas chamber, hanging, and firing squad.

Since 1976, when the Supreme Court allowed states to reinstate the death penalty, ninety-five people on death row have had their convictions overturned through the analysis of DNA and other measures. If these figures are typical of the rate of wrongful conviction, one in eight prisoners now on death row aren't guilty of the crimes they were convicted of.

It costs approximately $660,000 to send someone to jail for life and $2 million to run a death penalty through the U.S. court system.

fourteen

Justice, Injustice, and Everything in Between

"Injustice is relatively easy to bear; what stings is justice."

—*H. L. Mencken, satirist*

Filmmaker Errol Morris made the film *The Thin Blue Line* about convicted murderer Randall Adams. The movie, in essence, presented the felon's innocence and resulted in his being freed from prison. In gratitude, Adams promptly sued Morris for using his story to make money. They settled out of court.

Once a patron of the country and western bar Bobby Mackey's Music World in Wilder, Kentucky, sued for $1,000 damages for being, in his words, "punched and kicked" by a ghost in the men's bathroom. Case dismissed.

Astronomer Carl Sagan sued Apple computers in 1993 for using his name as an in-house code name for one of the computers they were developing, a long-standing tradition of respect at Apple. Apple designers went ahead and changed the name Sagan to BHA while it was still in development. Carl learned what the new name stood for—"Butt-Head Astronomer"—and sued again for defamation. This time he lost.

A TM (Transcendental Meditation) follower once sued the TM Society and a top guru because the plaintiff was never able "to achieve the perfect state of life they promised." One of the agreements he felt was broken was that the group had promised he could learn to levitate. He claimed he only learned to "hop with the legs folded in the lotus position." He was awarded $138,000 in damages.

In 1878 James McNeill Whistler sued art critic John Ruskin for libel after a scathing review. He "won": Ruskin had to pay him a farthing—about a quarter of a cent.

With a tip of the hat to Henry Ford's assembly line invention, Supreme Court Chief Justice Charles Evans Hughes made this observation: "The United States is the greatest law factory the world has ever known."

Sanity may be counted now as a legally protected class, thanks to the case of *Woods v. Phoenix Society of Cuyahoga County*. When Mr. Woods, a clerk, was fired from the mental health agency, the Phoenix Society of Cuyahoga County, because a background search revealed he did not have a past history of mental illness, he sued his employer. He was the only employee at the agency without a history of mental illness, and the courts agreed that he was entitled to sue on the grounds of reverse discrimination.

Voltaire reflected, "I was never ruined but twice: once when I lost a lawsuit, and once when I won one."

John Scopes, if you remember, actually lost the Scopes evolution (or "monkey") trial and was convicted of unlawfully teaching evolution. It was, however, reversed on a technicality.

Dr. Samuel Mudd, ancestor of newsman Roger Mudd, was unjustly convicted of helping conspirators. He unwittingly helped set the broken leg of John Wilkes Booth while Booth was on the lam for killing Abraham Lincoln.

Two months after boxing promoter Don King was acquitted of fraud, he packed up and took the jurors who acquitted him on a trip to the Bahamas.

Sob Story

In 1956 Liberace sued the London *Daily Mirror* for libel for suggesting he was gay. Despite the fact it was true, Liberace won. Damages paid were court costs plus 8,000 pounds. Liberace brazenly claimed that the name-calling hurt so much he "cried all the way to the bank."

In 1983 Liberace wasn't so lucky in court: A young man named Scott Thorson, who was on Liberace's payroll as bodyguard and chauffeur, sued for $113 million in palimony. Although there was never a ruling because the case was settled out of court, Thorson, by all accounts, walked away with some (maybe all) of what he was asking for.

"Law never made men a whit more just."
—*Henry David Thoreau, author*

The ACLU sued NYC mayor Rudolph Giuliani seventeen times between 1994 and the end of 1998. They won fifteen times.

Alger Hiss was the first lawyer in Massachusetts to be readmitted to the bar after being disbarred. A victim of the communist "Red scare," his fine reputation rehabilitated him in 1975.

Native Americans, diplomats, even Minnesotans in canoes can freely pass between Canada and the United States. But Cajuns—once known as "Acadians" before they were expelled from Canada by the British from 1755 to 1762—have specific legal restrictions based on their history as French-speaking forced exiles.

"Nobody wants justice."

—Alan Dershowitz, lawyer

fifteen

The Root of All Evil

My goodness! Your dear old uncle seems to have left everything to __me__!

"A man may as well open an oyster without a knife, as a lawyer's mouth without a fee."

—*Barten Holyday,*
seventeenth-century playwright

The average portion of money awarded by the courts that gets consumed by legal costs is about 54 percent.

Puck magazine had this to say: "Ignorance of the law does not prevent the losing lawyer from collecting his bill."

In 1964 a tourist sued San Francisco, claiming that a minor cable car accident had turned her into a nymphomaniac. She won $50,000.

In 1985 an ex-Coke employee filed a lawsuit against the company for firing her. She won a $600,000 settlement. The reason for her termination? "Conflict of interest," said the Coca-Cola Company: She had married a Pepsi employee.

If there's a discrepancy between the dollar amounts on a check, the bank can legally honor the written-out amount.

"Defending the underdog is fine, but it's usually the upperdog who can pay the big fees."

—*Alfred Hitchcock, on the television show* Alfred Hitchcock Presents

Excessive money-grubbing can run you into trouble. In 1998 the sporting goods company Adidas had a lawsuit slapped on it, not from disgruntled customers or employees but by a Chinese labor camp detainee. It seems the ultra-low-bid companies that contracted to provide Adidas with their official World Cup '98 soccer balls had used prisoners to make the balls. Political activist and prisoner Bao Ge filed suit upon his release against the sports company, claiming he was forced to stitch balls or be beaten.

"The Crime of '73" was a name given the 1873 revision of the U.S. coinage laws. Up until that point the silver half-dime was made up of 20 grains of Pure Grain

Standard Silver. From that date on, no silver was used at all in production.

Sometimes contracts have less to do with money than with brown M&Ms. In David Lee Roth's autobiography, *Crazy from the Heat,* the band member clears up the legendary "brown M&M clause" of Van Halen's performing contract. (It stipulates that a bowl of M&Ms with the brown ones removed must be provided backstage.) The clause is in there, he admits. But primarily as a test to make sure promoters and production teams read the technical specifications of the band's elaborate concerts, also in the contract.

You'd think lawyers would know better: Presidents Andrew Jackson, Ulysses Grant, Abraham Lincoln, and James Garfield all died without wills. The leading expert and promoter of wills, Thomas Jarman, died without one, too.

In his will Ben Franklin left 2,172 pounds, 5 shillings to his son-in-law, Richard Bache, with the one stipulation that he set free his slave, Bob.

The Green-Eyed Monster: Patrick Henry of "Give me liberty or give me death" fame left all of his estate to his wife in his will. There was only one catch: In order to receive it, she could never marry again.

Henry expounded, "It would make me un-happy to feel I have worked all my life only to support another man's wife." Ditching the money, she remarried.

In contrast, poet Heinric Heine stipulated that his widow *must* remarry before inheriting his estate. As reason, his will reads, "So at least one other man will regret my death."

Author and lawyer Robert Louis Stevenson once had a dear friend who was born on Christmas. She was forever complaining of never having a real celebration. So being a good friend, upon his death, Stevenson willed her his birthday.

A well-known Canadian lawyer, Charles Millar, whimsically left a large portion of his estate to the woman in Toronto who would have given birth to the most children in the decade after his death. Half a million was split equally between four women who each bore nine children in that time frame.

A wealthy Connecticut woman named Helen Dow Peck believed in Ouija boards. While she was using one, her hands on the board spelled out that she should leave her entire estate to a man named John Gale Forbes. The only problem was that she didn't know anybody by that name. In fact, after she died in 1956, her lawyer did a search throughout the world and discovered that, despite the all-knowing spirits, there was nobody with that name.

sixteen

Law by the Numbers

"**5**0/50: That's the chance that a person charged with homicide in the United States will be convicted of the crime.

A little less than half of all lawsuits end up in court.

40,000: The number of liability lawsuits filed in the United States every year. That compares to about 200 filed every year in the United Kingdom.

See that law textbook or the huge brief sitting on your desk? If typical, 13 percent of the letters in it are *e*'s. Don't believe us? Then go on and count 'em.

In the United States, there are about 220 law schools. Of these, 175 have been approved by the ABA (American Bar Association) or the AALS (Association of American Law Schools), the two governing bodies of the legal profession and law training in the United States.

$38,000: How much it costs per year to attend Harvard Law School.

55 percent: The portion of new law graduates that take their first jobs with private law firms. The other 45 percent accept first jobs with the government, corporations, or outside the legal field altogether.

12 percent: That's the number of law graduates who take jobs outside the legal profession.

70: The number of words per minute a good legal secretary should be able to type.

$35,563: The average salary a legal secretary can expect per year for typing that fast.

69,000: The number of lawyers in Washington, D.C. That averages out to about one in eight residents of the city.

The number of lawyers in the United States doubled between 1970 and 1985.

2/3: The portion of the world's lawyers who practice in the United States.

1 in 10,000: The lawyer-to-citizen ratio in Japan.

1 in 1,000: The lawyer-to-citizen ratio in England.

1 in 356: The lawyer-to-citizen ratio in the United States.

$300 billion: That's how much Americans spend annually on litigation.

When the American Bar Association was established on August 21, 1878, there were 100 lawyers who made up its membership. Today there are more than 350,000 members.

New York State sees the most malpractice lawsuits against individual physicians. They also have the highest number of personal injury attorneys.

You've Come a Long Way, Baby: Forty-three percent of the general counsel who run the Fortune 500's legal departments are female. More than half of those women have been hired since 1996.

Still a Long Way to Go: Less than 2½ percent of the general counsel who run the Fortune 500's legal departments are minorities.

20,000: The number of telephone records subpoenaed every year in the United States.

28 percent: The percentage of TV news directors who say they've dropped "important information" from a story for fear of being sued.

seventeen

Life Outside the Law

Saint Augustine admitted to many acts of depravity in his famous *Confessions*. One of them was, "I studied law and considered becoming a lawyer."

Actor/comedian John Cleese's other profession? He's a lawyer.

True Story: Tchaikovsky really wanted to be a lawyer but "settled" for composing instead.

Harry Lillis Crosby, accompanied by the consternation of his family, dropped out of law school to sing and play the drums. Harry, also known as Bing, did alright.

If you up and dropped your law career, you'd be in good company. Check out some of these one-time lawyers who reformed and took up honest work: Fidel Castro, Mohandas Gandhi, Erle Stanley Gardner, Francis Scott Key, Vladimir Ilyich Lenin, Geraldo Rivera, Noah Webster, Robert Lewis Stevenson, and Charlie Rose.

Did you know that besides his famous legal work, lawyer Clarence Darrow wrote a fictional novel, *An Eye for an Eye* (1905)? It tells the story of a poverty-ridden man named Jim Jackson who murders his wife in a fit of rage.

What was *Jarndyce v. Jarndyce*? The name of the lawsuit in *Bleak House,* Charles Dickens's satirical look at a family fighting over inheritance.

During the 1940s a California attorney started the Court of Last Resort—an organization that helped people who were wrongly imprisoned. The lawyer's name was Erle Stanley Gardner, and before he dedicated his life to writing stories about the legal hero Perry Mason, he was known for defending poor Mexican and Chinese immigrants in the California legal system.

Perry Mason made his literary debut in 1933 in *The Case of the Velvet Claws.* Gardner wrote seventy-five *The Case of the . . .* books. His last, in 1965, was *The Case of the Troubled Trustee.*

Henry Fielding, the author of the classic *Tom Jones,* was a lawyer. Amazingly, he received his law degree in three years, when, in his day, it normally took students six or seven.

Lew Wallace, author of *Ben Hur* and other books, was an attorney. His credibility was destroyed when he took up the pen. He once commented, "I might as well have appeared in court dressed in a clown suit."

Supreme Court Justice Byron White had another career before law: He was the NFL's top rusher in 1940. Also known as "Whizzer," White played for three years with the Pittsburgh Pirates before beginning his career in the legal profession. He now holds a place in the Football Hall of Fame.

Steve Dallas, one of the minor human characters in the *Bloom County* comic strip, was not just the songwriter extraordinaire of such hits as "Let's Run over Lionel Richie with a Tank," and "Heck's Bells" for the amazing band "Billy and the Boingers." He was also, first and foremost, a lawyer who managed the ragtag band.

"Georgia on My Mind" and "Stardust" were written by lawyer/songwriter Hoagy Carmichael.

Consider the private lives of the famous musical writing team of Gilbert and Sullivan: Arthur Sullivan was a pious man who wrote "Onward Christian Soldiers"; in contrast, William Gilbert was a barrister.

In the famous Gilbert and Sullivan song "Ruler of the Queen's Navy," from the opera *H.M.S. Pinafore,* a job as an attorney's office boy ("polishing up the handle of the big front door") qualified the character for becoming ruler of the queen's navy.

People who were lawyers before they became famous in other fields: TV sportscaster Howard Cosell, singer Julio Iglesias, and writer Washington Irving.

Otto Preminger was a lawyer before he directed movies like *Exodus, Porgy and Bess,* and *The Man with the Golden Arm.*

Outlaw John Wesley Hardin, who also invented the shoulder holster, practiced law in his spare time.

Gandhi was a lawyer. On one occasion this fact gave Winston Churchill enough rope to hang himself in the annals of history: "It is alarming and also nauseating to see Mr. Gandhi, a seditious Middle Temple lawyer, now posing as a fakir of a type well known in the East, striding half-naked up the steps of the viceregal palace . . . to par-ley on equal terms with the representatives of the king-emperor."

"**I** learned law so well, the day I graduated I sued the college, won the case, and got my tuition back."

—*Fred Allen, radio comedian*

"**T**he Star Spangled Banner" was written by lawyer Francis Scott Key. He was negotiating the release of a client from a British navy ship when a battle broke out and he was trapped aboard. The nighttime battle so stirred his soul that he wrote down the patriotic words and later put them to the tune of the British drinking song "To Anacreon in Heaven."

Just Desserts: It was a California attorney named Logan who initially crossbred berries to produce the loganberry during the late 1850s.

Before he entered the food business, Colonel Harlan Sanders, of Kentucky Fried Chicken fame, studied law through a correspondence college.

Star-Studded Cast: Dick York (later famous as the husband on *Bewitched*) played a young Tennessee schoolteacher/ defendant. Frederic March played the prosecutor, Spencer Tracy played the defense attorney, and Henry Morgan, the judge. The movie was *Inherit the Wind,*

based on the story of the 1925 Scopes
Evolution Trial.

In the early 1900s U.S. Navy man Carl
Haffke talked his way into becoming king
of a little known principality near the
Philippines named Ilocanos. It was a
step up; before that, he'd been a court
stenographer.

About two-thirds of America's presidents
have been lawyers.

The following presidents have one thing
in common—they all dropped out of law
school: William McKinley, Teddy

Roosevelt, Woodrow Wilson, Franklin D. Roosevelt, Harry Truman, and Lyndon Johnson.

Attorney Abraham Lincoln patented both a perpetual motion device and a buoyancy device for rescuing ships that were caught on shoals in 1849. Neither got beyond the drawing-board stage.

It's a well-known fact that none of the founding fathers who were lawyers actually went to a school of law. Thomas Jefferson helped open the doors of the first law professorship in the United States, at the college of William and Mary in 1779.

Although not going back as far as the founding fathers, Strom Thurmond (Republican senator from South Carolina) was a successful lawyer who also never went to law school.

Dracula was a lawyer. Sort of. Dracula—or Vlad the Impaler—ran an entire court almost single-handedly. He often played lawyer, judge, jury, and executioner.

Another Reason to Hate Lawyers: The Society for the Preservation and Encouragement of Barber Shop Quartet Singing in America was founded by an attorney in Tulsa named Owen C. Cash in 1938.

eighteen

Take It from Me...

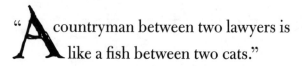

"A countryman between two lawyers is like a fish between two cats."

—*Ben Franklin*

Consider the Amish: They will neither initiate lawsuits nor defend themselves against them.

"It ain't no sin if you crack a few laws now and then, just so long as you don't break any."

—*Mae West*

"One lawyer can steal more than a hundred men with guns."

—*Mario Puzo, from his novel* The Godfather

"Love is the fulfilling of the law."

—*Romans 13:10*

"How to win a case in court: If the law is on your side, pound on the law; if the facts are on your side, pound on the facts; if neither is on your side, pound on the table."

—*Unknown*

"Good men must not obey the laws too well."

—*Ralph Waldo Emerson, poet*

"Never look too deep into the mind of a lawyer."

—*Brisco County Jr.,*
on the TV show The Adventures of B. C. Jr.

"You know what I say. Whenever you got business trouble the best thing to do is to get a lawyer. Then you got more trouble, but at least you got a lawyer."

—*Antonio Pirelli in the 1939 Marx Brothers movie* At the Circus

"The only way you can beat the lawyers is to die with nothing."

—*Will Rogers, writer/commentator*

Acknowledgments

The authors wish to thank, first and foremost, that lawyerly fellow Bruce Aitken for being enthusiastic about our ideas. Also to our fearless editor, Leslie Berriman, and her faithful sidekick, Heather McArthur.

Thanks to Brenda Knight for taking us to her leader, and to Pam Suwinsky, the finest wordsmith around. Also: Anthony Petrotta, Jennifer McCormack, Gloria McCracken, and Gillian Shepherd. Warm "hellos" to Jackson Hamner, E-lana Mingo, Georgia Hamner, Eric "Stumpy Joe" Childs, and an appreciative nod to Elaine Harrison, Esq.

Selected References

Books

Anchor Bible Dictionary, ed. David Noel Freedman. Doubleday & Company, 1992.

The Book of Answers: The New York Public Library Telephone Reference Service's Most Unusual and Entertaining Questions, by Barbara Berliner with Melinda Corey and George Ochoa. Fireside Books, 1990.

A Book of Legal Lists: The Best and Worst in American Law, by Bernard Schwartz. Oxford University Press, 1997.

The Compact Edition of the Oxford English Dictionary. Oxford University Press, 1985.

The Completely Amazing, Slightly Outrageous State Quarters Atlas and Album, by the editors of Klutz. Klutz, Inc., 2001.

Curious Punishments of Bygone Days, by Alice Morse Earle, 1896.

Encyclopaedia Britannica, ed. the faculties of the University of Chicago. Benton Publishing, 1979.

Funny Laws, by Earle and Jim Harvey. Signet, 1982.

The Guinness Book of Records: 1999, by Guinness Publishing Ltd., Bantam Books, 1999.

Isaac Asimov's Book of Facts: 3,000 of the Most Interesting, Entertaining, Fascinating, Unbelieveable, Unusual and Fantastic Facts, ed. Isaac Asimov. Random House Value Publishing, Inc., 1997.

The Juicy Parts: Things Your History Teacher Never Told You about the 20th Century's Most Famous People, by Jack Mingo. Perigee Books, 1996.

Jumbo Quiz Book. Helicon Publishing Ltd., 1996.

Just Curious, Jeeves, by Jack Mingo and Erin Barrett. Ask Jeeves, Inc., 2000.

Law 101: Everything You Need to Know About the American Legal System, by Jay M. Feinman. Oxford University Press, 2000.

Medical Curiosities: A Miscellany of Medical Oddities, Horrors and Humors, by Robert M. Youngson. Carroll & Graf, 1997.

News from the Fringe: True Stories of Weird People and Weirder Times, compiled by John J. Kohut and Roland Sweet. Plume Books, 1993.

The Oxford Dictionary of Quotations, Third Edition, by Book Club Associates. Oxford University Press, 1980.

Panati's Extraordinary Origins of Everyday Things, by Charles Panati. Harper & Row Publishing, 1987.

The People's Almanac Presents the Book of Lists, by David Wallechinsky and Amy Wallace. Little, Brown, 1993.

Peter's Quotations: Ideas for Our Time from Socrates to Yogi Berra, Gems of Brevity, Wisdom, and Outrageous Wit, by Dr. Laurence J. Peter. William Morrow and Company, Inc., 1977.

Prime Time Proverbs: The Book of TV Quotes, by Jack Mingo and John Javna. Harmony Books, 1989.

Stories Behind Everyday Things: Strange and Fascinating Facts About What's All Around Us, by Reader's Digest. The Reader's Digest Association, Inc., 1980.

The 2,548 Best Things Anybody Ever Said, by Robert Byrne. Galahad Books, 1996.

2201 Fascinating Facts, by David Louis. The Ridge Press, Inc., and Crown Publishers, Inc., 1983.

Uncle John's Bathroom Reader, vols. 1–13, by the Bathroom Readers' Institute. Earthworks Press, 1988–2000.

An Underground Education, by Richard Zacks. Anchor Books, 1997.

Webster's New World Dictionary, Third College Edition. Simon & Schuster, Inc., 1988.

Webster's Unabridged Dictionary, Second Edition. William Collins & World Publishing Co., Inc., 1976.

Weird History 101, by John Richard Stephens. Adams Media Corporation, 1997.

Software

Microsoft Encarta 98 Encyclopedia. Microsoft, 1997.

World Book Encyclopedia. IBM, 1998.

Web Sites

American Bar Association, www.abanet.org

American Medical Association, www.ama-assn.org

Court TV Online, www.courttv.org

The Department of Justice's National Criminal Justice Reference Service, virlib.ncjrs.org/Statistics.asp

Electric Library, www.elibrary.com

Famous Trials by Doug Linder, www.law.umkc.edu/faculty/projects/ftrials/ftrials.htm

Find Law, www.findlaw.com

Lex Antica, www.members.aol.com/pilgrimjon/private/LEX/LEX.html

Paul Revere House, www.paulreverehouse.org

U.S. Department of Labor/Bureau of Labor and Statistics, Occupational Outlook Handbook, stats.bls.gov/ocohome.htm

U.S. Supreme Court Multimedia Database at the Oyez Project, Northwestern University, oyez.nwu.edu

Useless Information, home.nycap.rr.com/useless/contents.html

Wholepop Magazine Online, www.wholepop.com

About the Authors

Jen Fariello

Erin Barrett and Jack Mingo have authored twenty books, including *How the Cadillac Got Its Fins, The Couch Potato Guide to Life*, and the bestselling *Just Curious Jeeves*. They have written articles for many major periodicals, including *Salon, The New York Times, The Washington Post*, and *Reader's Digest* and generated more than 30,000 questions for trivia games, and—from their new home in Charlottesville, Virginia—studiously avoided any activity that involves lawyers.

You can contact Erin and Jack at:
ErinBarrett@earthlink.net
JackMingo@earthlink.net

To Our Readers

If you would like to receive a complete catalog of Conari books, please contact us at:

CONARI PRESS

An imprint of Red Wheel/Weiser, LLC

368 Congress Street, 4th Floor
Boston, MA 02210
617-542-1324   fax: 617-482-9676
www.redwheelweiser.com